CONSCIOUS FOOTSTEPS

CONSCIOUS FOOTSTEPS

An intense unravelling.
A return to self.
A walk back to truth.

Dion Elliott Jensen

CONSCIOUS
IMPRINT

First published in Australia in 2025 by

Conscious Imprint Pty Ltd
PO Box 300
New Farm QLD 4005
ABN 98 690 850 027

conscious-imprint.com

Copyright © Dion Elliott Jensen 2025

The right of Dion Elliott Jensen to be identified as the author of this work has been asserted by him in accordance with the *Copyright Amendment (Moral Rights) Act 2000*

This work is copyright. Apart from any use as permitted under the *Copyright Act 1968*, no part may be reproduced, copied, scanned, stored in a retrieval system, recorded, or transmitted, in any form or by any means, without the prior written permission of the publisher.

A catalogue record for this book is available from the National Library of Australia.

ISBN 978 1 7643119 0 8 (paperback)
ISBN 978 1 7643119 1 5 (eBook)

Cover design by Conscious Imprint
Interior design by Conscious Imprint

Printed and bound in Australia by INGRAM®

For Mackenzie, Lachlan, Sienna, Isabella, and Eva – the most important pieces of me.

May each step you take be guided by light, love, and purpose. For whether you're conscious of it or not, you'll leave a footprint with every step you take.

May we live forever in peace,
free from the shadows of our memories
and from the fears of our future.

CONTENTS

Walk 1 *Death of an Ego*
Walk 2 *I Am Who I Am, Not What I Do*
Walk 3 *Controlled by Fear*
Walk 4 *Life Sentence*
Walk 5 *Love Is a One-Way Street*
Walk 6 *You Never Know Your Last*
Walk 7 *Stay for a Minute, a Month, or a Lifetime*
Walk 8 *The Stories We Are Told*
Walk 9 *Reborn Again*
Walk 10 *Authentic Love*
Walk 11 *Spiritual Growth in a Material World*
Walk 12 *The Purpose of Love*
Walk 13 *Endless Summer*

PREFACE

This book wasn't written in one sitting. I've been walking it for a lifetime.

Some pages were typed through tears. Others arrived as quiet truths whispered in the stillness. Some even came to me as I slept, in my dreams. This book came together slowly, moment by moment, breath by breath, step by step.

This is not a manual. You won't find checklists or ten-step formulas here. Just one life. One story. One soul's memoir of its unfolding journey through the edges and depths of being human.

Yes, my name is on the cover, but I come to you not as someone known. This is my first book. There's no platform behind these words, no fame, no following, no bias—just a willingness to tell the truth.

That anonymity removes distraction. When we know too much about someone, it's easy to project or compare. But when we don't, we're left only with the words and perhaps the space to meet ourselves in them.

Each chapter in this book is a walk. An intentional pause. An invitation to step out of the noise of daily life and into presence. You're not expected to read it all at once;

PREFACE

in fact, I hope you don't. Let each walk be just that: a moment of movement, reflection, stillness. An invitation to take it with you on a literal walk. Let it breathe. Let it settle. Let it echo in the quiet places.

As we walk together, take only what feels right, what resonates, what aligns with your experiences, or even gently challenges you. As for the rest, don't discard it. Those may simply be walks meant to be taken another time.

This isn't a beginning or an end. It's a meeting point.

Where you go from here is entirely up to you.

But if you choose to walk...

I'll walk with you.

WALK 1: DEATH OF AN EGO

WHEN THE WORDS OTHERS CHOSE TO DESCRIBE ME WITH WERE DIFFERENT FROM MY SPIRIT, I KNEW IT WAS TIME TO DIE.

I hear the laughter of children, pure and unfiltered joy echoing through their play, their voices alive with the sacred rhythm of being. I close my eyes, and even in the stillness of winter, I can feel the gentle kiss of the setting sun upon my skin. I can receive this now. I can be present with it.

But why did I have to die for me to truly appreciate it?

It was not a swift death. It was slow. Painfully slow. A long, intense unravelling, from the first brutal blow to the final shallow breath. It stretched across five relentless years.

My ego fought hard. It had built the entire scaffolding of who I thought I was, my personality, my worth, my existence. And yet looking back, it was all so fragile. So easily shattered and tenuously held together by grit, relentless will, and the constant need to endure. To fight and achieve and, most importantly of all, never fail.

"I am successful. I am wealthy. I am happy. I am desirable," it would scream, like a warrior in a battle that never ended.

Life became a scoreboard. Look at my house. Look at my car. Look at the places I dine. Look at what I own. Always chasing more. Always needing more. More. More. More.

But beneath the noise, my spirit whispered. It longed for something deeper and more meaningful. I yearned for connection, for peace, and for truth. I craved acceptance, but I couldn't even be honest with myself.

It was November 2019. On the surface, everything appeared in perfect alignment. My career had given me a title that made me feel powerful, seen, and significant. The compensation was generous. The respect was palpable. I was married to a kind, beautiful, brilliant woman. We had two incredible daughters. We travelled the world and lived a life most would envy. By every external measure, I had won.

And then, in a single breath, it was gone. I was fired.

CONSCIOUS FOOTSTEPS

The period that followed was nothing short of traumatic. My identity, every thread of my being, had been intricately woven into that role. My ego was tethered to it completely. And in a single, brutal moment, it was all stripped away.

I was left exposed, raw, and unanchored. Worse still, the life I had built, our home, our lifestyle, the security I provided, was all dependent on what that role afforded. Now, it all hung in the balance.

I was terrified. But I was not alone.

And I, and my ego, chose to fight.

By some divine timing, we had a holiday pre-planned for the very next day. My wife, our two young daughters, and I flew to Hawaii. We carried more than luggage. We brought fear, uncertainty, and the heavy silence of the unknown. But we also carried each other.

The bond my wife and I shared became our strength. The girls gave us purpose, a reason to hold steady. And the same grit and fierce will I had always relied upon when my fragility surfaced came rushing in to carry me through.

I wanted to use the time to reflect, but my ego, wounded and humiliated, wrestled with the truth of being fired. I couldn't even say the word. It caught in my throat like a stone. My voice would falter, my body would tighten, and my heart would race. I felt naked. Ashamed. Like I had failed not just myself but my family. I imagined the eyes of strangers on me. There he is, the one who got fired. The shame ran deep.

Perhaps the hardest part was the betrayal I felt toward myself. I had carefully crafted a life, a perfect image. One that justified every decision, every sacrifice. And in a moment, it shattered.

In my mind, I had become nothing. I had no job, no income, and worse, I had unknowingly outsourced my worth to a title, a corporation, a system that never truly sees people and individuals. I had traded authenticity for approval. Now, stripped bare, all that remained was the question: *Who am I, without all of it?*

Everything I had in life, I had earned. I didn't come from wealth or privilege. I watched my Mum struggle to put me through school, and by the age of seventeen, I had stepped into the role of provider. I accepted it without question; it seemed like a natural progression.

That role carries a quiet, constant pressure. In some past relationships, I began to feel that it was the role being loved, not the person behind it. That realisation was hard to face. It fed the ego, yes, but it wounded the heart and spirit deeply.

During this time, I was incredibly fortunate to have the unwavering love and support of my wife's family. They showed up emotionally, and my sister and brother-in-law offered financial support as well. Their generosity lifted a significant weight and allowed us to keep our home and preserve a sense of stability for our young family.

But for someone so used to being the one who provides, my ego took another hit.

I applied for countless jobs. The responses were few. Each time I had to explain the sudden end to my last role, it felt like a shadow I couldn't escape. The weight of rejection began to build.

In time I made a choice: rather than continuing to chase roles that no longer felt right, I would start my own business. I knew I had the skills. More than that, I wanted to reclaim control, to rebuild on my own terms, and to repay the generosity of those who had supported us as quickly as I could. It was no longer just about recovery. It was about reinvention. And, in truth, about rebuilding the ego I had lost.

I was successful. My ego wants me to write that. To be fair, I always believed I would be. Making money had never felt particularly difficult. I used the skills I had, built a solid business, and repaid the generosity that had helped us get back on our feet. I had big dreams. I saw the business as a future unicorn, ready to take on the world. It was unique, with little competition, and all signs were pointing in the right direction.

Then Covid hit.

The world came to a halt. More specifically, the world stopped travelling. And for a business predicated on people travelling, that was a devastating blow.

My ego began to dread the question, "How's the business going?"

Whether it came from family, friends, or former colleagues, at a barbecue, or at the school gate, it all felt the same. My ego convinced me they already knew it wasn't going well, and they were just twisting the knife.

I prepared a stock response: "Oh, it's going well, thanks. More importantly, how are you?" Deflection, after all, is easy once you get someone talking about themselves.

It took a long time for me to see what was really happening. The shame I carried from being fired, combined with the pain of a struggling business, had built invisible walls between me and others. My ego was the builder. It stood between me and my authenticity, blocking the spirit of who I really was.

I began to understand that not every question is a judgement. Sometimes, people are simply asking because they care. The role my ego was playing became clear. It was no longer protecting me. It was holding me back from being myself.

With that awareness, I started noticing the same patterns in others. The world had shifted. Covid forced many to re-evaluate their lives, changing careers, moving homes, slowing down. Isolation brought introspection, and in that quiet space, people began to question what truly mattered. I began to see just how deeply our egos are tied to the roles we perform, and how letting go of them is the first step toward truly becoming ourselves.

With Covid behind us, I turned my attention back to my career, which, if I were honest, still meant my ego was chasing money and success. Our family unit was strong, and the girls were growing quickly. Life had a rhythm again.

When I first met my wife, our connection felt alchemic. Friends would often comment on the depth and intensity between us, saying it was something extraordinary to witness. That bond, that unshakable connection, has been a constant example of strength and fortitude, and was something I remain deeply grateful for.

We had always communicated well, openly and with respect. Our love for each other ran deep. But sometimes the universe has plans different to ours that we don't foresee. Cracks had begun to appear. Both of us carried frustrations, quiet tensions over different needs and expectations going unmet. They weren't enough to break us apart on their own, but instead of facing them, we let the distractions of daily life create a kind of wilful blindness to them.

One day, we were talking about a news article I had come across, a piece on the idea of an annual marriage break. I shared it as something of interest, and it opened the door to a broader conversation. And within that space, an innocent question emerged. One that would change the entire trajectory of my life.

The article explored a growing trend in parts of Europe where couples in long-term marriages were experimenting with the idea of taking a one or two-week break each year. The intention was to step outside the daily structure of the relationship and pursue individual interests, whether that be travel, creative pursuits, social experiences, or even sexual exploration. It was framed as time to reconnect with oneself, free from the considerations of the other partner.

During our conversation, she asked me what I would do with my annual break. I spoke openly about the places I would travel to, and without hesitation, mentioned that I might also be curious about exploring sexual openness.

In response, she half-joked, "Oh, I'm sure you would have fun with..." followed by the names of three random women.

I replied, "Well, I might also find and have fun with an Adam."

I can still see the look on her face, her eyes wide, stunned, like someone caught in the high beams of an oncoming car. In that instant, the cracks we had both been avoiding could no longer be ignored. My stomach dropped. I felt sick. Yet beneath the fear, I also knew I had just spoken a truth that had lived unspoken inside me for a long time. My heart was pounding. It was the first time I had ever hinted, to anyone, that I was sexually attracted to men.

Let me be clear, I don't for a moment want or need you to think I wasn't genuinely attracted to or deeply in love with my wife. As I've said before, our connection has always been alchemic, otherworldly even. A soul bond that I truly believe transcends this world.

But I had been carrying my desires like a weighted vest for forty-one years. They had never been spoken. Never acted upon. Never allowed into the light of day. That same weight pressed down on my self-worth and inflated my need for external acceptance.

When I spoke those words to her, I stumbled, fumbled, and tried to pull them back as quickly as they'd escaped.

But it was too late. They were out. And just like that, without planning, without preparation, I had taken my first step toward coming out as my authentic self.

The months that followed were a whirlwind of emotion. At times I felt anticipation, excitement, and hope. At others, I was consumed by fear, shame, grief, anxiety, and deep sadness. I was watching the life I had built and rebuilt and the identity I had clung to slowly fall away. Yet at the same time, I was stepping into something more real. Something that had waited quietly inside me for three decades.

Up to that point, everything I felt was rooted in emotions alone. I hadn't acted on any of my same-sex attraction. I only knew that the yearning and desire had always been there. Years of living as a hetero-normative male had confused and clouded my inner truth. I struggled to imagine what life might look like if I allowed myself to live as a gay man. It felt foreign and unfamiliar.

But what I did feel, perhaps for the first time, was a sense of alignment. A quiet knowing. A feeling of rightness.

The energy my ego had needed to maintain the version of me the world saw, to wear my mask, had been draining. And as that identity began to dissolve, it made way for something new. An energy that wasn't about survival or performance but discovery. The energy to finally meet myself, as I truly am.

I will always owe my ex-wife an immeasurable debt of gratitude. As I moved back and forth between the two versions of myself, as my ego gasped for its final breaths, she stood strong in her values and beliefs.

I wanted to stay. I offered to silence the true version of me that was finally ready to emerge, to continue living the life we had built together as a family. But she, with deep knowing, said no.

Instead, she spoke words, that while said to me, I hope will guide our daughters one day:

"We can't be together, because all of me, isn't enough for you."

In that moment, something shifted. Her strength gave me permission to honour the truth I had spent a lifetime hiding. I was finally free to be me.

But even as the scaffolding of my ego collapsed, I discovered the roles it had built were still clinging to me. I was no longer a straight man with a title, yet I was still asking myself, who am I?

WALK 2: I AM WHO I AM, NOT WHAT I DO

I CARE TO KNOW YOU, NOT THE MASK YOU WERE TAUGHT TO WEAR TO BELONG IN A WORLD THAT DOESN'T RECOGNISE YOU.

My job title only served two purposes. First, to feed my ego. Second, to signal to others how I might be of use to them, which in turn circled back to serve the ego once again.

Think about any time you meet someone new, at a barbecue, a networking event, or any social gathering. After the usual greetings, silence will inevitably ensue and the next question is almost always some variation of, "So, what do you do?"

And just like that, the exchange shifts to a conversation between masks. We speak through the polished veneer of our title or role, filtered through layers of bias, expectation, and assumption.

We are conditioned to place certain roles on pedestals. The doctor, for example, may be revered without anyone knowing of the pain they inflict through domestic abuse behind closed doors. The Uber® driver may be often overlooked or looked down upon, while their flexibility allows them to spend their time volunteering at an orphanage and they live a life rich in service, purpose, and alignment.

Our titles are not who we are. They are costumes in a play we've been cast into, often without question. The soul speaks quietly beneath them, waiting to be heard, waiting to be asked... *Who are you?*

I am who I am, not what I do. That became my quiet mantra.

To put it into practice, I set myself a challenge. Whenever I met someone new, I'd ask, "Tell me about yourself...but don't tell me what you do for work." The reactions were almost always the same. Silence. Confusion. People didn't know how to answer, let alone where to begin.

One by one, they stumbled. It made me wonder, do most of us not know who we are beneath the roles we perform? Some would say, "I'm a father," or "a mother," "a husband," "a wife," as though domestic roles define us any more than professional ones. But then, someone responded with a question of their own. One that stopped me in my tracks.

"Tell me who you are?" they asked.

And just like that, the question I had been asking of others turned back toward me, and it cut deeper than ever before.

"Umm...good question," I laughed awkwardly, trying to buy time as I searched for an answer. Eventually I responded, "To be honest, I don't really know. I'm still working that out."

Even though my ego had spent years dying and my authentic self had begun to emerge, I still didn't fully understand who I was. More importantly, I hadn't yet uncovered what I truly valued, how I wanted to show up in the world, or how I wished to be seen. The version of me that was real, unmasked, and unguarded still felt like a stranger.

I'm a thinker, at times an over-thinker. I've come to see it as both a gift and a challenge. The question *'Who am I?'* echoed in my mind for months. I found it easier to articulate who I was not. And strangely, it was through that contrast that I began to find alignment. In shedding what didn't fit, I started to feel into what did.

One of the greatest challenges I faced in the death of my ego was realising just how deeply my identity had been tied to my work. My sense of self, the version of me I showed to the world, was built almost entirely around what I did. So, when I was fired, I didn't just lose a job; I lost myself. Without the title, I felt like a nobody. Unworthy. To myself and, as I imagined it, to others as well.

I've since observed how common this attachment is, especially among men in the corporate world. And while I write generally here, it extends far beyond the workplace. It shows up in families too. Women become mothers, and in that role, they often lose sight of who they are beyond it.

Please don't get lost in the gender roles I've referenced; that's not the point.

The point is this: I am who I am, not what I do. And neither are you.

Watching young children interact is a powerful lesson in authenticity. They engage with the world and each other in a way that is pure, unfiltered, and free. Until we begin to teach them otherwise, they carry no bias, no judgement, no masks. There are no preconceived ideas, no need to perform. Just presence. Just truth.

When a child meets another, you'll often hear something beautifully simple: "Hi, my name is... I'm this many years old... I like this... I don't like that..." They don't see race or religion. They don't apply labels or bias. They connect soul to soul. Their sense of self is steady and untouched, until the world tells them it should be something else. Until the world gives them their mask.

That's what happened to me.

Somewhere along the way, I learned that who I was needed to be polished, presented, and positioned. I traded wonder for work ethic. I replaced curiosity with caution. And I convinced myself that value comes from usefulness, not presence.

When I stopped identifying with what I did, I was left with silence. And at first, it was uncomfortable. Without a title to hide behind, I had no script to read from. But in that stillness, something else began to speak, a quieter truth. I began to notice what lit me up. What drained me. What felt like alignment. What didn't. It wasn't instant. It wasn't always clear. But it was real.

I started to rebuild not a new identity, but a new relationship with myself. One that didn't rely on achievement or admiration. One rooted in honesty. I began to remember what joy felt like without needing to earn it. I began to trust myself again.

And I came to understand something simple but life changing. I don't need to be *someone* to be *me*.

We live in a world that keeps asking us to explain ourselves. To prove our value before we've even spoken. But beneath all the roles, all the armour, all the polished responses, there is someone real. And that's enough.

So, if no one asked what you do, if you couldn't point to a title, a role, or a task...who would you be?

When the mask falls, you expect freedom. But sometimes, what you meet in the silence beneath it isn't clarity; it's fear. Fear that perhaps without the mask, there's nothing of value left. And that was the fear I couldn't escape.

WALK 3: CONTROLLED BY FEAR

HELL, FOR ME, IS A PLACE WHERE THE NOW IS LOST BENEATH THE WEIGHT OF WHAT WAS AND THE FEAR OF WHAT MIGHT BE.

The best way I can describe the limitations I placed on myself is through the image of concrete boots. Heavy with fear, they held me in place. I couldn't move forward, backward, left, or right. I was stuck. And there I stayed.

Days passed. Then weeks. Then months.

Nothing changed, except my age.

Fear wears many faces:

Fear of failure.

Fear of rejection.
Fear of lack.
Fear of the unknown.
Fear of death.
Fear of losing control.
Fear of not being good enough.
Fear of being judged.
Fear of change.

I was afraid. Constantly. At times I still am. Afraid of losing everything. Afraid I won't be able to provide for my family. Afraid there won't be enough. I once had grand visions—dreams of wealth, freedom, and expansion—and before I could ground them, they were replaced by the most primal fear of all: survival.

'Let's design and build our dream home' became 'Can I cover the rent?'

'We should try that hot new restaurant' became 'Will I be able to put food on the table?'

I was overwhelmed with frustration. My ego screamed, "How could someone with so much potential, so much drive and ambition, so much experience, and so many past achievements feel so powerless?"

My heart broke; my eyes wept. I felt shattered.

I hated how much I depended on others to feel successful. Even my best intentions, my plans, my business dreams, still relied on clients and customers. I had handed them the keys to my happiness without even realising it.

I also resented the dependence others had on me. My generosity, once given freely, had become a crutch for others and a chain for me. Guilt kept me there. The desire to preserve relationships kept me there. I was being controlled, not by people but by my own self-imposed fear.

Money, or more precisely, the fear of not having enough of it, was my kryptonite. Not just money itself, but the consistency and security I believed it promised. Just beneath that fear was another: the fear of not being in control.

Life teaches us to plan. Business teaches us to plan. If you fail to plan, you plan to fail is a commonly heard mantra. But what is a plan, if not an attempt to control an outcome? And what if that outcome refuses to be controlled?

I was always good at planning. Goal setting was second nature. I could map out a path and I would climb, step by step, like each part of the path was a rung on a ladder, the destination clear at the top.

But lately, with every rung I climbed, it felt like my foot slipped. The goal remained, but the path beneath me was crumbling.

Deep down, I knew I no longer wanted the corporate life. When I see office buildings now, they feel like prisons. Not metaphorically. Literally. Glass-fronted cages where presence and purpose are traded for security. We enter them in our twenties, often full of promise and ambition, and before we know it decades have passed.

We trade our daylight hours for direct deposits. We measure life in promotions and performance reviews. We come in early, stay late, skip lunch, smile politely, and learn to suppress everything that doesn't serve the role or the company. Companies that, in truth, don't even exist outside of human invention. Abstractions, legal fictions, and registrations made real only by our collective belief in them.

We give our freedom in exchange for financial security. And for a while, it feels worth it. We justify it. We need the money. We want the title. We convince ourselves it's just for now. Just until the mortgage is paid, just until the next milestone, just until we can finally slow down.

But we rarely do.

The system isn't built to let us off the treadmill. It's built to keep us moving quietly, efficiently, obediently.

When the world shifted in the aftermath of the pandemic and work-from-home became the norm, many of us got a glimpse of what we'd unknowingly surrendered. Time. Autonomy. Presence. We remembered what it felt like to cook a meal in the middle of the day, to walk barefoot outside after a meeting, to pick up or drop off our children from school.

We remembered how good it felt to breathe.

I don't believe the answer is to burn it all down, but perhaps it is to begin again. Consciously. To choose work that aligns. To create outside the system. To shift the way we measure value. To walk slowly, not out of fear but out of intention.

That is the shift I am still learning to make.

Fear hasn't vanished. It still whispers, still tries to tie concrete boots to my feet. But alongside it, there is something else. Even in my most anxious moments, I can feel it: a heartbeat, a flicker, a quiet presence that feels like hope.

And hope is what begins to crack the concrete, loosen fear's grip, and remind me that the prison I feel is one of my own making and therefore, one I can walk free from whenever I choose.

I'm reminded of a question someone once asked me in a moment of fear and uncertainty. It still echoes today:

"If you knew you couldn't fail, what would you do?"

For years, that question felt like pressure, another demand to perform.

Now, it feels different. Hope flickers when I hear it.

WALK 4: LIFE SENTENCE

WE BUILD THE CELL WALLS IN THE PRISON OF OUR MIND, AND IT IS THERE WE SENTENCE OURSELVES FOR LIFE.

Our minds are incredibly powerful instruments, capable of both healing and harm. They can protect us, justify our actions, fuel endless speculation, reinforce limiting beliefs, or slowly wear down the very body they inhabit. The mind can be a vast open ocean, a tranquil forest, or a prison of our own making.

How can the same mind that dreams, creates, invents, and loves also be the one that depresses, isolates, and contemplates its own end?

That's the question I found myself asking. Because at one point, I wasn't just battling fear. I was starting to believe it might be easier if it all ended.

The mind doesn't whisper only once. It loops. It replays. It finds every angle, every worst-case scenario, and every regret, and hits repeat. Over and over again.

You're not enough.

The worst outcome is a foregone conclusion.

You're running out of time.

You've failed.

It's too late.

Everyone can see it.

They're just being polite.

You should be further along by now.

You're the problem.

The repetition makes it feel true. Familiarity begins to feel like fact. And the more the thoughts loop, the more they dig in, carving grooves into the landscape of the mind like skis through fresh snow. They become harder to interrupt and even harder to challenge.

Unfortunately, I am a repeat offender. I have been incarcerated and released by my mind many times. In the court of internal dialogue, the prosecution has a commanding presence, one that often catches the defence off guard and under-prepared. The judge and jury seem to have no choice but to convict.

I remember one moment clearly, in one of the darkest corners of my mind's prison cell. I was driving home, tears streaming down my face. The same thought looped again and again: *How did I get myself to this place?*

My body was the scoreboard of the physical manifestation of my imprisonment. Sleep fractured. Jaw clenched. Head pounding.

In desperation, I called out to something greater. I screamed through tears, to whatever force was listening, "*I give up!*" Again and again, louder and more desperate each time. Until the scream tore through my throat and left it raw.

In the silence that followed, I felt a shift. Not because the circumstances had changed, but because I had finally let go. I had surrendered. And in that surrender, I found a sliver of peace. Not because I had figured it out, but because I had stopped trying to control it.

Since then, I no longer see my thoughts as facts. They are visitors. Some stay too long. Some arrive uninvited. But none of them are the whole truth.

I am learning to meet them differently. To listen without attachment. To challenge the stories that no longer serve me. To offer myself compassion instead of judgement.

I still fall. I still stumble. The courtroom of my mind still opens from time to time. But now, when the prosecution shouts its case, I am learning to bring my spirit to the witness stand.

Perhaps the greatest shift has come not in silencing the mind, but in how I choose to see.

Because what I perceive, I believe.

What I focus on, I feel.

What I expect, I often experience.

My perception is my reality.

This is not instant. It is practice. A slow retraining of the lens through which I view the world. Some days, I see through fear. Other days through hope. Sometimes through love, sometimes through lack. But whatever lens I choose, it shapes what I see. And where my energy goes, my life flows.

The prison of my mind was real. The walls were heavy. The sentence felt final. But the greatest realisation of all was this. The key had been with me the whole time. With each moment of awareness, with each breath of compassion, I learn that I can turn it, step through the open door, and walk free.

WALK 5: LOVE IS A ONE-WAY STREET

I LOVE NOT TO BE LOVED BACK. I LOVE BECAUSE IT REFLECTS MY SOUL.

Show me a love that is truly unconditional, and I will show you a reflection of the soul at its purest. A love that remains, even in silence. A love that holds its ground when unrecognised. A love that gives because it cannot do anything else.

Before I truly understood this, I would look at my dogs and wonder. Could this be what unconditional love looks like?

The happiest part of their day, without question, is when I come home. Whether it's been five minutes or five hours, the greeting is always the same. Wagging tails, affectionate eyes, excited whimpers, bodies vibrating with joy. It isn't about where I've been or what mood I'm in, if I've had a bad day or snapped at the world.

They just love. Fully. Freely. Without condition.

It's one-way, but it never feels lacking. Their love isn't transactional. It doesn't rely on performance, attention, or return. They don't love because I'm perfect. They love because I'm theirs. And in doing so, they remind me what love is meant to be: pure, expressive, and without expectation.

We say, "I love you." And often, we hear or expect to hear in return, "I love you too." But what if that echo never comes back? Would your love diminish? Would it dissolve? Is your love reliant on it being received and returned?

Is there even such a thing as unconditional love? Or have we diluted its meaning by attaching it to people we expect might fail us?

To say, "I love you unconditionally" is often a preemptive defence. It implies, "Even if you hurt me, I will still love you," rather than, "I love you with no need for you to love me in return."

True one-way love isn't about tolerating pain. It's about transcending the need for love to be transactional. It's about finding peace in knowing that the love you give says everything about you, and nothing about whether or not it is mirrored.

CONSCIOUS FOOTSTEPS

Should you ever find someone who can love this way, quietly, fully, freely, hold them close, or better yet, become that person. Because in being that person, you will know love that is not bound by time, by reciprocation, or by ego. You will know love as it was always meant to be.

I remember the last time I ever saw my Dad. I was eleven, nearly twelve, and had just returned from being overseas with my Mum for about eight months. I hadn't seen or spoken to him the entire time we were gone. Looking back, I don't even know if he knew where we had gone or why. My parents had separated and eventually divorced in the years prior.

It was lunchtime, and I was playing in the schoolyard with my friends when he showed up at the gate, asking to see me. A teacher came over and asked if I wanted to go to him. I said no. Not because I didn't want to see him, but because I was enjoying the moment with my friends. I didn't understand that there wouldn't be another opportunity.

Time moved on. I grew up. I lived my life. I became a father myself, having my first child, a daughter, one month after turning twenty-one. Over the next few years, I was blessed with two more, a son and another daughter. Over the same period, my dad had remarried and built a new family of his own.

Eventually, my first marriage ended in a messy, painful divorce. The kind that leaves scars deeper than most people care to admit. It irreparably fractured the family unit, left biased narratives in its wake, and created confusion for our children, their innocent hearts caught in the middle of the crossfire.

Yet through that pain came something unexpected. A seed of clarity. I began to understand my father in a way I never could as a child. I began to challenge the story I'd been told about him. I started to consider the possibility that the version I had accepted might not have been the whole truth.

I was travelling for work when the urge to reconnect with him grew too strong to ignore. I sat in a shopping centre food court and opened my laptop. With nerves in my hands and hope in my heart, I wrote:

"Hi Dad, it's Dion. I've been through some life experiences that have made me reflect. I'm starting to realise that what I've been told may not be entirely accurate. I'd really love the chance to reconnect. Love, Dion."

A few days later, he replied:

"Hi Dion, it's nice to hear from you. But the pain of losing contact with you has been too great. It's not a wound I want to reopen. I don't want to reconnect with you."

As I read those words, tears streamed down my face. In that moment, my heart broke. Not just for me, but for the children I now found myself estranged from. My three eldest, whom I haven't spoken to for many years now.

I pictured their faces. Their childhood and teenage years that I'd missed. The memories we never got to make. I had fought so incredibly hard for them, for the right to see them, to be part of their lives. But that fight became something else. It turned into a battle for validation. It became about being heard, being right, being seen.

I longed not just to love them, but to be loved back. I wanted my love to be realised, returned, confirmed.

But love, true love, doesn't demand those things. That's what I began to understand.

Love doesn't shout to be acknowledged. It simply waits. Quietly. Faithfully. Completely.

This realisation isn't about giving up. It's not about making peace with the silence just to survive it or finding a way to appease the ache of missing them. It's about something far more sacred. It's about surrendering the fight, not the love. It's about honouring the purity of what I feel without tying it to an outcome.

My love for them doesn't need their presence to exist. It doesn't vanish in their absence. It simply is.

This isn't weakness. This is strength in its most enduring form, a love that doesn't close, doesn't fade, doesn't condition itself on being returned. A love that waits, with arms always open, not because it expects but because it knows no other way to be.

It was in that moment I made a vow. Should any of them ever return, no matter how many years had passed, no matter the silence, no matter the pain I'd carried in their absence, my door would—will—remain open. Always. Not for a moment will it close. My love will be there. Unwavering. Patiently waiting.

That was the moment I truly understood what unconditional love meant.

True love does not require reciprocation. It doesn't withhold affection until it's been earned. It doesn't come with conditions or timelines. True love gives without asking anything in return. It flows in one direction, not because it must, but because it can.

Because it is.

This kind of love is rare. In a world that often trades affection like currency—"I love you if…" or "I'll stay if…" or "I'll give, but only if you give back"—unconditional, one-way love is a radical act. It defies ego. It defies logic. It breaks every rule we've been taught about self-protection.

It is also the only true form of love, because it comes from within.

It is not a response; it is an offering.

I love you.

WALK 6: YOU NEVER KNOW YOUR LAST

OUR FIRSTS ARE FILLED WITH EXCITEMENT; OUR LASTS ARE FILLED WITH LOVE. THE ART OF LIVING IS TO FEEL THEM BOTH AT ONCE.

We celebrate our firsts.

Our first steps.
Our first words.
Our first kiss.
Our first job.
Our first love.

We remember them; we mark them; we hold them as milestones. They become part of our story, and rightly so. Firsts carry weight because they signal beginnings.

But somewhere along the way, as life gathers speed, we stop noticing. The ordinary becomes background noise. We move through days without realising that every moment carries the potential to be our last.

The last bedtime story.

The last school drop-off.

The last time you hold someone's hand as their partner.

The last conversation you didn't know was goodbye.

The truth is, we rarely know our lasts until they've already passed us by. They slip quietly into memory, and we only see them in hindsight. If we had known, we would have clung tighter. We would have lingered longer. We would have tasted the moment for all it was worth.

I think of the last time I saw my father. I didn't understand that I was saying no to my last chance. I didn't know that memory would echo for decades as the final moment we would share.

I think of the last time I kissed my ex-wife as her husband. Neither of us knew, in that instant, that it was the final kiss of our marriage. A thousand kisses before, and yet that last one slipped by unnoticed, carrying with it an ending neither of us could yet name.

I think of my eldest children, the last time I saw them before silence replaced presence. I didn't know it was the end of that chapter. If I had, I would have held their faces in my hands, told them everything I wished I had said, and refused to let go. But I didn't know. I thought there would be another tomorrow, another moment. And then, there wasn't.

And then, there is him, my fiancé. We met at a time when I was still carrying the ache of my own lasts, but I didn't yet know that he was carrying his too. On our very first date, the conversation turned to this idea of not knowing your last.

I told him about my children, about how I didn't realise the last time I saw them would be the last for the foreseeable future. I spoke from my own pain, not knowing how deeply it would land. Only later did I learn that he had very recently lost his Dad. What I was sharing wasn't just reflection but a mirror to his own heartache. My words touched a wound still raw. I hadn't known, and yet somehow the conversation found him exactly where he was.

It showed me again how universal this truth is. We all carry our own lasts. Some we recognise too late. Some we never saw coming. Some we hold with gratitude; others with regret. But all of them remind us of the same lesson. To be here now.

Because if we don't know our lasts, then the only way to truly live is to treat each moment as if it could be. Not in fear but in reverence.

The last sip of coffee you don't rush through but taste.

The last sunrise you don't just see but watch unfold.

The last laugh with a friend you don't cut short but lean into.

The last breath you take without knowing it's the final one.

Presence is not waiting for significance to appear. Presence is seeing the significance in what is already here.

We spend so much of life in the elsewhere, caught between the shadows of the past and the projections of the future. We replay what has already gone, or we plan what may never come. Meanwhile, the present slips through our hands unnoticed.

The mind is loud. It wants us to live everywhere but here. It tells us you'll be happy when this happens, safe when that comes, fulfilled when you finally reach that destination. But life doesn't exist in those places. It only exists here, in this breath, this step, this heartbeat.

Imagine if you knew this was your last day. How would you move through it? Would you still be scrolling on your phone? Would you still hold back the words you long to say? Would you still rush through your morning, blind to the colour of the sky, deaf to the sound of the birds, numb to the softness of a hug?

Or would you let yourself be drenched in the fullness of it all as though every sense, every detail, mattered?

That's the invitation of presence. Not to fear the end but to honour the now.

We can't change the past. We can't predict the future. But we can live differently now. We can choose to see every "ordinary" moment as extraordinary. We can treat today's simple, fleeting gestures as if they might be the last because one day, they will be.

CONSCIOUS FOOTSTEPS

And when that day comes, when a chapter closes or a life shifts, we will know we didn't waste it. We will know we showed up. We will know we were here.

Every laugh.
Every hug.
Every goodbye.
Every sunrise.
Every footstep.

All of it is precious. All of it is passing. All of it is a chance to be fully alive.

And perhaps that is the point. To live as though every moment matters. To love as though it could be your final chance. To stay awake to the truth that nothing is guaranteed, and presence is the only way we truly honour life.

Some people, some moments, some seasons, you don't know if they're here for a minute, a month, or a lifetime. All you can do is meet them fully, as though each could be your last.

WALK 7: STAY FOR A MINUTE, A MONTH, OR A LIFETIME

THANK YOU FOR BEING PART OF MY JOURNEY. OUR CONNECTION IS NOT MEASURED BY TIME BUT BY THE MOMENTS WE TRULY WALKED TOGETHER.

We often think the strength of a relationship lies in its duration. The friend we've had for twenty years must be more important than the one we've known for two. The partner we've been with the longest must be the one who knows us best. But time is a poor measure of truth.

CONSCIOUS FOOTSTEPS

Some of the deepest, most impactful relationships in my life lasted only a season. Some taught me more in a single chapter than others did across an entire volume.

The truth is that relationships are not bound by time. They are bound by presence. By impact. By the authenticity we bring to them. Every connection has a reason, a season, or in rare cases, a lifetime.

Across our lives, the roles people play shift with the seasons we're in. As children, our world revolves around our parents or caregivers. Then friends arrive and feel like everything. Later, teachers and mentors begin to shape our worldview. As we age, romance adds depth, complexity, and vulnerability. Work relationships sometimes take centre stage, bound not just by task but by shared intensity. Parenthood re-frames everything again. The roles evolve. People come in and out. Some stay. Some fade. And some remain only in memory.

The illusion of permanence is one of the great traps we fall into. We expect the closeness we have with someone today to remain unchanged tomorrow. But the soul doesn't work like that. We are meant to grow, to evolve, to stretch beyond the known. Some people are sent to walk only part of our path with us. They were never meant to stay. And that's okay. Their exit does not erase their impact.

Then there are the sacred, fleeting encounters. The stranger on a plane who tells you the exact thing you needed to hear. The short-lived friendship that sparked something lasting. These are just as important. Not all teachers stand in a classroom. Not all angels have wings.

Some appear for a moment, shift something within us, and vanish.

But in all relationships, whether momentary or enduring, authenticity is the key. When we mask who we are, whether through fear, shame, confusion, or the simple fact we haven't yet met our true self, the relationships we build attach to the mask, not to us.

They reflect the version of ourselves we believe is safe to present. And while that may protect us in the moment, it leaves us unfulfilled because to be loved as the mask is to remain unknown.

Masking doesn't just limit how others see us; it limits how we experience love. There were seasons in my life where I was hiding, even from myself, whether it was out of fear of being vulnerable, fear of judgement, or even not yet knowing my own truth. I wore a mask. I wore the mask of the achiever, the provider, the confident one, the partner who had it all together. But inside, there were parts of me quietly crying out to be known.

When we live in concealment, we starve our relationships of truth. We attract people to our performance, not to our essence.

And sometimes, those masks are born from survival. A child learning that vulnerability leads to punishment. A teen hiding their identity because it's unsafe. An adult conforming to norms they never chose.

Each mask once served a purpose, but at some point, if we want real connection, we have to choose to put the mask down.

Relationships built on truth are liberating. They hold a mirror to our soul. Sometimes they reflect our light. Sometimes they expose our shadows. But always, they serve a purpose. They guide us, challenge us, heal us, or humble us. And when we surrender the idea that relationships must last forever to matter, we begin to see their beauty for what it is: not permanence but presence.

Endings, too, can be sacred. We don't talk enough about the art of release. Sometimes love means letting go. Sometimes walking away is the highest form of respect, for yourself or for the other. It does not mean what was shared was wrong or broken. It means its purpose has been fulfilled. Holding on too tightly can distort the memory, making the ending bitter instead of beautiful.

The grief of outgrowing someone is real. So is the ache of realising a bond that once defined you can no longer hold who you've become. That pain deserves space. It deserves compassion. But it does not mean the relationship was a failure. It means you've changed. And that change is sacred.

The real gift of connection lies not in ownership but in experience. What if every person you met, whether friend, partner, colleague, or even adversary, was a mirror? A soul chosen to show you something vital. A reflection of your growth. A lesson your spirit came here to learn.

Seen through that lens, even heartbreak becomes a teacher. Even betrayal becomes a mirror. Even silence has wisdom in it. We stop asking, "Why did this happen to me?" and begin asking, "What was this here to show me?"

There is freedom in this way of seeing. It allows us to honour each relationship for what it was, not what we wished it to be. It teaches us that we are not made whole by another, but that we come into relationships whole and hopefully leave them with more of ourselves intact, not less.

This is the sacred dance of souls, not to possess but to witness. Not to cling but to cherish. Not to measure by time but by truth.

So, whether you stayed with me for a minute, a month, or a lifetime, thank you.

You were part of my becoming.

And I, perhaps, part of yours.

WALK 8: THE STORIES WE ARE TOLD

I WAS YOUNG AND IMPRESSIONABLE. I COULDN'T YET TELL FACT FROM FICTION OR KNOW WHICH OF YOUR STORIES WERE TOLD TO SERVE YOU AND WHICH WERE MEANT TO SERVE ME.

We are all shaped by stories. Some are told to us with love. Others with fear. Some come wrapped in wisdom, passed down from those who lived before us. But many, far too many, are created not for our benefit but for the comfort or protection of those telling them.

As children, we are like sponges, absorbing everything—not just words, but tone, silence, glances, body language. We're wide open, forming our view of the world and our place within it. And so, the stories we're told in these formative years become the foundations of our identity, regardless of whether they're true.

One of the most damaging environments for these distorted narratives is found in relationship breakdowns. Two people, once bound by love, now bound by resentment, begin to rewrite the script. In the name of self-preservation, or sometimes revenge, parents shape their version of events and pass it on to their children as truth. They cast themselves as the victim, the other as the villain. In doing so, they don't just fracture the relationship; they fracture a child's sense of reality.

Children in these situations are often forced to carry the weight of stories they never asked to hear. Stories that aren't theirs to hold. Stories that place them in the middle of an emotional battlefield confused, conflicted, and too young to make sense of the war around them. Their loyalty is tested. Their voice is silenced. Their innocence is quietly sacrificed at the altar of adult ego.

Worst of all, these stories can last. They linger. They harden. A child might grow up believing a version of events carefully constructed to protect a parent's pain. It can take decades before the truth is uncovered, if ever. By then, damage has been done. Relationships are strained, worldviews distorted, and the child, now grown, must sift through the debris to find their own voice again.

This walk is for those children. The ones who grew up questioning their memory. The ones who lived under someone else's version of reality. The ones who wonder if love should feel this conflicted, this conditional, this full of silence and sides.

It is also for the parents who may find themselves tempted to rewrite the past to ease their pain. Let this be a reminder, your child deserves the truth—and not your version of it but the space to find their own. Your role is not to weaponise your story but to protect theirs.

And importantly, this walk is for anyone brave enough to look at their life and ask, "Whose story have I been living? And is it even mine?"

From the age of twelve, I was told my father wanted nothing to do with me. When my parents divorced, he refused to pay child support, so my Mum didn't allow me to see him. I wasn't encouraged to speak to him or have a relationship with him. I was told he would speak badly about her when I was with him, yet I had no memory of that.

Then, without warning, I was taken overseas for eight months. No contact. No explanation. At the time, I was too young to understand what was happening. I just accepted it as truth.

Years later, I found myself on the other side of a very similar story.

In the aftermath of my own divorce, my three eldest children were suddenly gone. I fought with everything I had: court cases, legal battles, desperate pleas for access. But no matter how hard I tried, I couldn't undo the power of a story told often enough.

A new narrative had taken hold. One that painted me as unfaithful, disinterested, and undeserving of their love. I was vilified. And my children believed it. I was shut out, cut off and alienated as their father. The pain was like nothing I had ever known.

It wasn't until I lived through this experience myself that I began to question the story I had been told about my father. And I came to realise it wasn't all true. The story I had grown up with wasn't about what was best for me; it was about protecting a parent's pain. It was a defence mechanism, not a foundation of truth.

This walk isn't about blame. It's not about pointing fingers or shaming anyone. It's about understanding how deeply our lives are shaped by the stories others tell us and how often those stories have little to do with us, and everything to do with the storyteller.

It's not just families that tell stories. Entire systems do.

Religion tells us stories about heaven and hell, good and evil, who we are and what we're worth. Some of these stories offer comfort, structure, and meaning. Others instil shame, fear, and division. The child who questions is often silenced. The one who doesn't fit the mould is told to repent, to conform, to erase the parts of themselves that make others uncomfortable. Spirituality becomes performance. Morality becomes control. And the story isn't about divine connection; it's about obedience.

Society tells us who we're supposed to be. What success looks like. Who to love. When to marry. What a 'real man' or 'proper woman' should be. It builds expectations so deeply into our psyche that we don't even realise we're following a script someone else wrote. We chase achievements we never wanted. We seek approval from people we don't respect. We sacrifice joy for appearance and authenticity for acceptance, and we vilify those who don't conform.

Schools tell stories about intelligence, potential, and failure. A child labelled as disruptive, lazy, or slow may carry that story into adulthood, long after the teacher has forgotten their name. And the education system rarely makes space for curiosity outside the curriculum, or for gifts that don't fit neatly in a box.

Even friendships and workplaces are built on unspoken narratives. We're told who's popular, who holds power, who we need to be in order to belong. And so, we contort ourselves and we adapt. We shrink or exaggerate parts of who we are to avoid judgement, ridicule, or being cast out. Over time, we forget what's real. We forget who we were before we learned who to be. We wear our masks.

The stories we are told then go on to shape the stories we tell ourselves.

"I won't be accepted."

"I'm not normal."

"I'm too much."

"I'm unlovable."

"This is just the way life is."

And perhaps the most dangerous of all:

"I am not enough."

Here's the thing: stories are powerful, but they are not absolute. They can be questioned. They can be rewritten. Just because someone once handed you a script doesn't mean you have to keep reading from it.

Some of the greatest healing in my life has come not from learning something new, but from unlearning what I was told.

At some point, often in a moment of crisis, pain, or awakening, we begin to hear a quieter voice. One that doesn't sound like our parents, our teachers, our leaders, or even our past selves. It is the voice of truth. Not universal truth, but personal truth. The kind that lives beneath the noise. The kind we buried for safety, then forgot how to find.

Unlearning is not a single act. It's a slow, deliberate unravelling. Like pulling on a loose thread and watching a tightly woven story come undone.

It begins with a question:

What if that wasn't true?

What if I'm not unlovable?

What if it's ok to simply be me?

What if success doesn't have to look like this?

What if I don't need to believe that to feel safe?

What if I start again?

One by one, the pillars of old stories begin to crumble. It's disorienting at first. When the foundations fall, what's left is unfamiliar terrain. But buried under the wreckage is something else, a compass. One that doesn't point to perfection or performance but to presence. To self.

CONSCIOUS FOOTSTEPS

You start to feel it when you speak your truth out loud and don't flinch. When you stop apologising for your boundaries. When you feel peace in your own skin, even if others don't approve.

Reclaiming your truth is not about being right. It's about being real. It's about learning to trust your own voice after years of hearing everyone else's more loudly than your own.

And something beautiful happens when you do.

You stop living to be chosen and start living as though you already are. You stop trying to make others comfortable and start getting comfortable with yourself. You stop chasing love and start embodying it.

This isn't arrogance. This is liberation.

The stories we were told may have shaped us, but they don't have to define us. And just as we inherited stories, we also pass them on. The more we live from our truth, the more permission we give others to do the same. Especially our children. Especially those still learning who they are in a world eager to tell them otherwise.

The stories we believe shape the world we see. Change the story, and the world changes too.

And so, we grow.

Not into who they wanted us to be.

Not into who we pretended to be.

But into who we've always been.

This process of returning to self is not loud. It doesn't always come with fireworks or declarations. Sometimes it comes in stillness, in realising you no longer react the same way to an old trigger. In recognising that your worth is not attached to being understood or validated. In finding peace not in what you've gained, but in what you've let go.

This is the sacred work of awakening and becoming.

It is not easy. It requires courage to question everything you were taught to believe about yourself and the world. It takes humility to admit that some of what you believed was never yours to carry. It takes strength to dismantle the constructs that once kept you upright, and to stand in your own truth instead.

But this work is freedom, and *your* truth will set *you* free.

Because when you rewrite the story, you reclaim the pen.

You become the author, not the character shaped by someone else's plot.

And from that place, life opens.

You speak differently. You love more honestly. You choose what serves your soul, rather than what satisfies an old script. You see others more clearly because you're no longer projecting the unhealed parts of yourself onto them.

The world hasn't changed, but your story has.

So, to those still trapped in someone else's version of you:

You are allowed to question and seek the truth.

You are allowed to let go.

You are allowed to rewrite.

CONSCIOUS FOOTSTEPS

The stories we were told were someone else's truth, but the story you live from now, that one is yours. Let it be honest. Let it be kind.

Let it be the story you needed when you were young.

Let it set you free.

WALK 9: REBORN AGAIN

THERE CAME A TIME WHEN I STOPPED SEARCHING AND STRIVING FOR WHO I BELIEVED I WAS SUPPOSED TO BE AND STARTED REMEMBERING WHO I ALREADY WAS.

My rebirth began not with fireworks but with fatigue. I was tired of performing. Tired of bending to fit someone else's mould. Tired of apologising for what made me different. At the core of that exhaustion was a quiet, aching truth; I no longer wanted to survive my life. I wanted to live and experience it, in all its glory.

For years, I clung to identities that once gave me purpose: the provider, the achiever, the husband, the father, the success story.

I was who I needed to be for others. I wore masks, played the expected roles, and carefully held together an identity that felt safe, even if it wasn't real. I was living in reaction. My identity was being shaped by those roles, expectations, and stories. I chased validation, approval, and belonging, often at the cost of truth.

Eventually, the façade began to crack, not through dramatic collapse but through slow, aching dissonance. An internal hum that said, *This isn't it. This isn't all of you.*

The old version of me needed structure and status to feel worthy. I built systems to hold myself up, based on discipline, order, output, validation. But structure without soul is a prison cell and I had built myself into one, brick by brick, convinced I was building a fortress.

As those identities started to unravel, I thought I was failing. In hindsight, I see now I wasn't breaking down. I was breaking open.

Rebirth came through dismantling, through letting go and realising that the world wouldn't end if I stepped outside the lines. That I wouldn't crumble if I admitted I didn't have it all figured out. That surrender wasn't weakness. It was sacred.

I began to reframe every challenge as a teacher. My relationship with control shifted. I began to see that control was often just fear wearing a tie. Fear of the unknown. Fear of not being enough. Fear of not being loved if I wasn't useful.

Letting go of control allowed me to see how deeply I had attached my worth to outcomes.

Rebirth and the journey to loving myself didn't begin with confidence or clarity. It began with honesty. It began when I stopped trying to become someone and started allowing myself to unbecome everything I wasn't. The grief of shedding those parts was real. They had served a purpose. They had protected me. But they were never truly me.

It felt like taking off a mask I had worn for years, stitched together from other people's expectations. I had been holding it in place so tightly, I forgot I could simply let it fall.

At first, I thought this would be a journey of becoming, of building something new. But I slowly realised that what I truly longed for wasn't something I could create; it was something I had to remember, to awaken to. To do that, I had to strip everything away.

That meant facing the truth of my own voice. My desires, my limitations, my sexuality, my pain. It meant making peace with the fact that I had hidden parts of myself, not because I was weak but because I didn't yet feel safe. I now understand that hiding was survival.

To live fully, I had to unlearn the deeply embedded belief that I was only worthy when I was achieving, pleasing, or performing. I had to surrender the exhausting cycle of self-improvement that was self-rejection in disguise. And perhaps hardest of all, I had to stop waiting for others to reflect my worth back to me before I could believe it for myself.

The unlearning was painful. Every belief I let go of had, at some point, offered comfort. They gave me structure, control, security, predictability. But they also kept me small.

I had to let go of the need to be the provider, the strong one, the one who had it all together. I had to be willing to disappoint people. To be misunderstood. To step out of the roles I had mastered and stand there, uncertain, honest, and whole.

In that process, my sexuality became more than something to accept. It became something to celebrate. I am a proud gay man. Pride didn't come easily, though. It came after years of silence, confusion, and shame. It came after realising that I had been living a version of myself edited for approval. It came after reclaiming my voice and deciding I didn't want to spend another day hiding.

I feel powerful in my truth now, not because it makes me better but because it makes me free. My sexual energy, once something I compartmentalised or suppressed, is now something I honour. It is vibrant, instinctual, alive. It is part of my wholeness, and I no longer apologise for it.

To love thyself is to integrate, to bring home the parts of yourself that were once scattered, shamed, or silenced. It is the willingness to hold your joy and your grief in the same breath. It is the courage to look at your past without judgement and your future without fear.

This chapter of my life isn't about reinvention. It's about reunion. A return to my natural state before I was told who to be. Before the world taught me to fragment. Before I learned to trade authenticity for acceptance.

It's also about releasing attachment. I no longer need to be understood in order to be at peace. I no longer need to control how others see me. My value is not up for debate. The constant striving to prove myself—in my work, in relationships, in identity—is falling away. In its place, there is stillness, clarity, and self-trust.

Loving myself has not made me immune to pain or uncertainty, but it has anchored me. When doubt arises, I no longer collapse. When fear visits, I can breathe through it. I return to the truth of who I am, and that truth holds.

I still carry dreams, and I still hold desires, but they no longer originate from a place of lack. They rise from abundance, from the overflow of knowing that I am enough. That I am already whole.

There are still shadows. There are still moments where old patterns tug at my sleeve. But now I meet them with compassion. I no longer exile the parts of me that are still learning. I invite them in, sit with them, and ask what they need.

Because love, real love, doesn't demand perfection. It demands presence. And loving myself is the most sacred presence I've ever known.

To love thyself is not arrogance, it is not resistance, and it is not ego. It is reverence. It is standing barefoot in the temple of your soul and finally saying, *Welcome home.*

CONSCIOUS FOOTSTEPS

I thought I was losing everything. But I was really making space, like clearing an overgrown garden, pulling up the weeds of outdated beliefs and finally letting the sunlight touch the soil.

I have now traded certainty for curiosity. I let wonder lead. I learned to hold questions without needing immediate answers. I learned to trust the unfolding.

Living in that truth gave me a kind of peace I had never known, a peace that doesn't come from everything being in its place but from finally being in mine.

I've begun to live from a place of abundance. Earlier in life, I lived with the constant hum of scarcity, scanning for what could be taken away, bracing for loss before it even arrived. Now I know the difference. I can feel it in my breath, in the way my shoulders settle, in the quiet that lives in my chest.

I used to think peace was the absence of problems. Now I know peace is the presence of self. It's the ability to hold space for everything—the joy, the fear, the grief, the longing—and still return to centre.

The past version of me built a life out of what he was told mattered. This version of me is building a life out of what feels true. A life that honours my spirit, not just my résumé and status.

Rebirth is a reclamation. It is the act of gathering every fractured part of yourself and welcoming them home. It is choosing love over fear, truth over performance, and presence over projection.

It is no longer needing to be seen as someone. It is simply being.

So, if you are in the in-between, no longer who you were and not yet who you will be, take heart. That's not confusion. That's emergence. That's the soil softening for something new to grow.

You are not broken.

You are awakening.

You are becoming.

And with every breath, you begin again.

WALK 10: AUTHENTIC LOVE

CAN YOU FEEL IT?
YES, I CAN FEEL IT. CAN YOU?
YES, I CAN TOO. I LOVE YOU WITH ALL MY HEART.

Love is not where my journey began. It's where I was led. After walking through the dark corridors of ego, fear, loss, and shame, I arrived somewhere softer. Somewhere more honest. I arrived in love. Not the kind we're taught to pursue or cling to, but the kind that rises naturally when nothing is left to prove.

Authentic love is the light that emerges when we stop hiding. When the masks fall away and we meet the world as we are, not as we were taught to be. It exists in every space we dare to be seen. And it changes everything.

We've been conditioned to confuse love with romance, with sex, with obligation. We fear expressing it too openly, too freely, in case it's misread, judged, or rejected. "I love you" is often weighed down by expectations or assumptions:

Are you in love with me?
Are you trying to cross a line?
Are you weak?

So, we withhold. We edit. We save love for sanctioned roles or safe containers. But what if love could just be love, a state of being, not a transaction? What if we stopped treating it as something scarce or exclusive, and allowed it to simply exist where it naturally arises?

There is love between friends that never touches the body but moves the soul. There is love between parent and child that teaches loyalty, sacrifice, and devotion. There is love with strangers, in passing glances, in shared laughter, in quiet kindness. And there is love within us, the kind that grounds, guides, and grows us.

All of these are real; all of them matter.

We've been taught to rank and restrict them, to believe one kind of love is superior, but I no longer believe that. Love is not linear. It has dimensions. Capacities. Rhythms. Some are soft and steady. Others arrive like lightning. And some, the most transformative, begin the moment we learn to love ourselves.

One of the most powerful examples of authentic love I've ever witnessed exists in the platonic friendship between my fiancé and one of his closest friends.

They met at work over two decades ago. She is a woman. He is a gay man. And perhaps because of that, society makes space for their closeness. It doesn't question it, doesn't assign it meaning, doesn't need to fit it into a romantic frame. But it's so much more than what society permits. It's deep, soul-rooted love.

The friendship is one-to-one, honest and complete. There is a shared history, a lived understanding, a willingness to witness each other completely. They share their lives, their stories, their heartbreaks, their wins, and their unravellings, openly, raw, without filters. They know everything about each other. There are no masks, no edits, no performances.

They live on opposite sides of the world, and the love doesn't diminish. They can go months without speaking, and the moment they reconnect, it's as if no time has passed. That, to me, is real love. A love that doesn't rely on proximity or performance but on truth.

Watching them has taught me something I didn't even realise I needed to learn. Friendship can hold just as much depth, devotion, and longevity as any romantic relationship and sometimes even more. Platonic love can be intimate. It can be sacred. It can be life-sustaining.

When I stepped into my truth as a gay man, I stepped into a new world of love. One where nothing needed to be hidden or translated. One where I wasn't performing or guessing what was "acceptable." It gave me the freedom to be me, and to express my love more freely.

Romantic love, when aligned with truth, feels like coming home. There's ease. Flow. Play. Intimacy that doesn't require effort, just presence. When I first realised this, it felt like something I could simply allow to exist. And I could get lost in it and lost to it.

With it came the most honest physical connection I've ever known. Sex wasn't a performance but an extension of emotion, of knowing, of trust. Roles didn't have to be fixed. At times I was held; at times I held. Power was exchanged not in dominance but in presence.

Authentic love allowed me to explore desire without shame. To inhabit my body without fear. To give and receive in full emotional and sexual honesty. It's the kind of love that feels like liberation.

One of the most powerful experiences of love I've had is with my ex-wife. Ours is no longer a romantic partnership, but the love that remains—the friendship, the co-parenting, the shared history, and mutual respect—is deep and enduring.

She supported me through one of the hardest transitions of my life, even though it meant the end of our marriage. That is a rare and generous love. We still walk beside each other, just on a new path. And that path is wide enough for gratitude, truth, and peace.

We parent our daughters with openness and presence. We laugh. We share. We support one another. And I will always honour the chapter we shared. Her love helped birth the man I am now.

Now, I choose to lead with love. In every space. In business, in family, in friendship, in intimacy. I no longer fear that love will be misunderstood, diminished, or weaponised. I give it freely, not to get something back but because it's who I am.

There is strength in tenderness. Power in softness. And presence in letting yourself be fully seen. Love does not weaken us. It reveals us. It clarifies what matters and when we stop waiting for permission to love, we stop living afraid.

I no longer love to be loved. I love because it's what I came here to do.

Authentic love isn't something you chase. It's what you become when you're no longer hiding. It's what flows from the heart when the walls come down. It's not reserved for the few. It's available to all.

Lead with love. Trust where it takes you. Speak it. Live it. Offer it. And let it remake the world around you.

Because when love is real, it doesn't need to be earned, only recognised.

WALK 11: SPIRITUAL GROWTH IN A MATERIAL WORLD

SPIRITUALITY IS NOT FOUND IN WHAT YOU OWN OR WHAT YOU REJECT...BUT IN HOW LIGHTLY YOU HOLD BOTH.

For a long time, I thought being spiritual meant turning my back on material life. That to grow inwardly, I had to reject outward comfort. I believed spirituality was reserved for those who meditated on mountaintops, who renounced wealth, who spoke only in riddles and revelations.

To be spiritual, I thought, was to be removed, untouched by ambition, disconnected from desire, above the world in some way.

But that idea never quite fit.

I liked nice things. I liked beautiful homes, great food, luxury travel. I still do. And for a time, I judged myself for that. I believed my love for the material disqualified me from the spiritual. Worse, I judged others too, either for having too much or too little, for flaunting or for rejecting.

The truth is, I didn't yet understand the real heart of it all. Spirituality isn't about what you own but how what you own owns you.

When I was fired, as I shared in Walk One, it wasn't just the job I lost. It was the identity. The position. The paycheck. The lifestyle. And with it, all the material markers I had used to measure my value.

My ego had built a home in those symbols. I had convinced myself that the car I drove, the house I lived in, the clothes I wore—they were me. Or at least, they were how others saw me. And how others saw me, I thought, determined my worth.

So, when it all fell apart, I felt like I was dying. Not metaphorically. Literally. My nervous system reacted like I was under attack. My throat tightened. My chest constricted. I couldn't breathe. Underneath it all was the terrifying belief, *I can't survive this.*

The contrast was jarring. One month, I was flying first class, dining at high-end restaurants, living in a house that reflected my curated success. The next, I was borrowing money from my brother and sister-in-law to buy groceries and keep a roof over my family's head. I had gone from being the provider to relying on the generosity of others and with it came a shame so deep it stripped me bare. It forced me to confront how much of my identity had been built around what I owned and what I could give.

But I did survive.

And through that unravelling, I began to see clearly. I wasn't grieving the job. I was grieving the illusion. The belief that I was only as good as my output. That success, visible, tangible success made me someone.

Spiritual growth didn't come to me in a temple or while on a retreat. It came in the silence after the noise stopped. It came when I was stripped of the image and left with only the truth. And in that space, I met myself again. Not the polished version. The real one.

I came to understand that spirituality doesn't require poverty. It doesn't demand we reject wealth or ambition. It asks only this: don't confuse your worth with your possessions. Don't measure the depth of your soul by the size of your house. And don't mistake someone else's material life for a measure of their character or their connection to spirit.

A car doesn't tell you who someone is, a watch won't tell you if they love deeply, and a postcode won't tell you if they're kind. These things are not irrelevant, but they are also not defining.

I've seen the damage that comes from over-identifying with material things. I've lived it. I've felt the fear and lived the reality of losing them. I've watched people chase them to the point of burnout, breakdown, and disconnection. And I've also seen the joy of having them, without attachment. Of enjoying beauty without ego. Of experiencing abundance without addiction.

It's not wrong to want a beautiful life. It's not wrong to desire financial freedom, success, and even luxury. But the danger is when we strangle the outcome. When we grip so tightly to one version of success, one path, one result, that we lose the flow of life.

Spiritual growth has taught me that it's okay to have dreams. It's okay to visualise and build and strive. But you must let go of needing it to happen in a particular way, at a particular time, with a particular label. You must let go of forcing and allow life to move through you, not just around you.

There were so many times I believed things had to unfold a certain way. That if I didn't reach a goal by a specific age or season, I had failed. That if I wasn't earning a certain income or living in a certain home, I wasn't enough.

That rigidity became a spiritual block. I couldn't hear my soul over the screaming of my schedule and goals.

So much of that belief system was conditioned in childhood. We're taught early on that material success is a proxy for worth. That having "made it" means living a certain kind of lifestyle. For some of us, scarcity in our youth made the pursuit of wealth feel urgent. For others, abundance created fear of losing what was never truly ours. Either way, it shaped how we valued ourselves.

Now, I see the truth more clearly. Money is merely a tool. A resource. A form of energy. It enables freedom. It supports wellbeing. It creates opportunity. But it is not the source of happiness. It is not the measure of meaning.

What's more, you don't have to be poor to be spiritual. Rather, you can build wealth and deepen your inner life and still be spiritual. You can fly first class and sit in stillness. You can walk barefoot in the sand and live in a beautiful home. One does not invalidate the other.

The key is consciousness. Intention. Awareness. Ask yourself, who am I becoming in pursuit of what I desire? Do my goals align with my values? Am I living in alignment, or am I performing again?

I no longer apologise for wanting nice things. And I no longer collapse if I lose them. My joy isn't tied to the leather seats or the ocean view. My joy comes from the peace within. From knowing who I am, regardless of what's in my bank account. That's the real wealth.

This new way of living also opened me to generosity. Not generosity for the sake of approval or for visibility or validation, but generosity as a natural outpouring of abundance. When you're no longer afraid of losing, giving becomes easy. Joyful. Sacred. I no longer hold tightly to money. I let it move, let it flow, let it serve.

There is also a peace in simplicity. Some of the most sacred moments in my life now are the quiet ones, the early morning walks, the stillness of reading, watching my children laugh, sharing honest conversation. These things don't cost anything, but they enrich me in ways no possession ever could.

We live in a world obsessed with comparison. Scrolling through curated snapshots of other people's lives, it's easy to forget that success isn't a universal metric. Someone else's abundance isn't a threat to yours. Someone else's spotlight doesn't dim your light. The true spiritual path teaches us not just how to manifest more, but how to appreciate what already is.

This chapter of my life is not about rejection. It's about integration. It's about living a grounded, abundant, generous life, without letting that life define me. It's about building, creating, and receiving while staying anchored to my truth.

And it's about remembering that the most valuable things in this world are often the ones that cost nothing at all. Presence. Kindness. Peace. Connection. Truth.

So yes, I will continue to dream. I will continue to build.

I will do so with open hands, not clenched fists. With gratitude, not grasping. With awareness, not addiction.

This is what it means to grow spiritually in a material world.

To walk lightly.

To live fully.

To be free with or without the things that once defined you.

And to know, in every fibre of your being, that you are already whole.

WALK 12: THE PURPOSE OF LOVE

THE PURPOSE OF LIFE IS NOT SOMETHING WE FIND. IT IS SOMETHING WE REMEMBER...TO LOVE.

There came a point in my journey when I stopped asking *What is the purpose of life?* and started hearing the quiet, undeniable truth that had been whispering all along. The purpose of life is to love.

Not the narrow version of love we've been conditioned to recognise, and not just romance, or passion, or the tidy lines of a relationship we can label and explain. Love in its truest form is so much larger. It is the nucleus of life, the current that sustains us, the energy that births, restores, and carries everything.

Love is the only emotion we are born with that needs no teaching. A baby doesn't learn to love its mother's touch or the warmth of being held. It simply loves. Everything else, we accumulate through life. Fear, greed, envy, jealousy, and hate are the products of conditioning. They are taught to us through the stories we are told and the masks we learn to wear.

In Walk Five, I wrote that love is a one-way street, the painful but liberating discovery that true love doesn't need to be reciprocated to exist. That realisation was the beginning of a deeper truth. Love is not just one way…it is *the* way. It is life's purpose itself.

The more I walked my own path, the more I saw that what strangles love is not its absence but our fear of it. Fear tells us love is dangerous, that to lead with it will make us weak, inappropriate, or foolish. Fear tells us love must be reciprocated to be real. But love, in its purest form, is never dependent. It simply *is*.

I had to unlearn so much to understand this. I had to shed roles, identities, and the façade that kept me safe but small. I had to stand bare in my truth, not as the provider, the achiever, the man hiding his sexuality, but simply as myself. And it was in that vulnerability that I began to see love not as something I had to earn or secure, but as something that had been flowing through me all along and something I was born with but had forgotten.

My Mum would tell me stories of when I was a child, and I can also remember moments myself, when I would see someone less fortunate. Without hesitation, I would begin to cry. I wanted to help them, to ease their suffering in any way I could. I was overcome with emotion, overcome with love. It was instinct. Pure. Unfiltered.

But there came a last time, a moment when I stopped responding that way. Somewhere along the way, I put on a mask. I stopped showing what I felt. I stopped letting myself be that little boy who could feel another person's pain and respond with love. Slowly, in a way that went almost unnoticed, I became conditioned not to.

Looking back, I see now that love never left me. It was still there, waiting beneath the mask. What changed was not love itself, but my willingness to let it be seen.

Over time, I had come to believe love had to be reflected back at me to exist, that it needed validation. My journey taught me the opposite. When I was estranged from my children, I discovered that my love for them did not diminish in their silence. It grew. It deepened. It became unconditional. That was when I realised love is one way. Love is not weakened by absence or silenced by rejection. Love is its own source, multiplying without limit as it is given and projected outward.

In saying that, here is the truth that many of us resist. We cannot love outwardly if we do not first love inwardly.

To love thyself is not arrogance; it is the foundation. Without it, every relationship becomes a transaction, a search for someone else to reflect back to us the worth we have not yet claimed. Without self-love, we live on borrowed approval, waiting for someone else to tell us we are enough.

Learning to love myself was the hardest part of all, because self-love required honesty. It required me to face my sexuality, my shame, my grief, and my fears without turning away. It required me to forgive the parts of me that I had hidden. To welcome home the parts that had been silenced. To see my own reflection and finally say: *You are worthy. You are enough. I love you (me).*

Self-love doesn't mean perfection. It doesn't mean I no longer stumble, or that old wounds never call my name. It means that when they do, I no longer exile them. I meet them with compassion. I sit with them. I remind myself that even in my shadows, I am whole.

When we live from that place, when love is not something we grasp for but something we *embody*, something changes. We begin to see love everywhere: in the laughter of friends, in the lessons of heartbreak, in the stranger who speaks a kind word, in the partner who holds us when we are tired of being strong.

Love exists in friendships, in family, in children, in community, in every connection where we show up authentically. And yes, it exists in romance too, in the deep alignment of finding a partner who sees the truest version of you, and in the ways intimacy becomes a sacred dance of giving and receiving, dominance and surrender, power and softness.

When I finally stepped into love that aligned with my true identity, it felt like breathing for the first time. Easy. Natural. Fluid. It was not about performance or fear. It was about presence. It was about truth.

The world teaches us to chase purpose like it's out there somewhere, hidden in careers, achievements, or accolades. But what if purpose isn't something to chase at all? What if it is simply to love, right here, right now, in the relationships we hold, in the work we do, in the way we meet strangers on the street?

What if every moment becomes an opportunity to embody love, to lead with it, to let it ripple outward in ways we may never see but that always leave a trace?

Love is not passive. It is not weakness. It is the most radical force we have. It dismantles fear. It disarms hate. It heals shame. It dissolves separation. It changes not only the world we live in, but the way we experience that world.

To live "on purpose" is to live as love. Not perfect love, not flawless love, but authentic love, messy, human, resilient, and enduring. Love that forgives. Love that releases. Love that holds. Love that is willing to risk being misunderstood because it refuses to be silent.

And so, when I say I now know the purpose of life, I say it with certainty...it is to love!

To love yourself enough to stand in truth.

To love others enough to see them beyond their masks.

To love the world enough to leave it better, softer, freer.

To live on purpose is to remember that love is both the beginning and the end of everything.

But I also know that for many, love feels out of reach, like an idea too big to grasp, too abstract to live. We've been taught to see love through narrow lenses, romantic gestures, dramatic sacrifice, or cinematic moments, while the truth is that love lives in the small. In the ordinary. In the daily choices we make without fanfare.

Love is listening without interrupting.

Love is holding the door open, even when you're in a rush.

Love is texting someone just to say, "I'm thinking of you."

Love is saying, "I was wrong," when your pride wants to be right.

Love is showing up, even when you're unsure how to help.

Love is asking, "How are you?" and meaning it.

It's a kind smile to a stranger.

It's folding the washing.

It's checking in with someone months after the funeral, not just the week of it.

It's putting your phone down and giving a person your undivided attention.

It's choosing patience with your child when they test every ounce of it.

It's forgiving, not for them but for your own freedom.

And love is also fierce.

It's saying no when something compromises your truth.

It's walking away from what no longer aligns.

It's setting boundaries that protect your peace.

It's resting, even when the world says grind.

It's being honest, even when your voice shakes.

And most radically, love is turning those same acts inward.

Speaking to yourself kindly.

Offering grace when you fall short.

Letting yourself rest.

Tending to your own needs.

Celebrating your own small wins.

Choosing not to shame yourself for still being a work in progress.

This is how love becomes a way of life, not through perfection but through presence. Not through grand gestures but through conscious steps.

In the previous walk, I explored the delicate balance between spirit and the material world, between survival and meaning, between the outer forms we need and the inner truth we crave.

What I came to see is that love is what makes that balance possible. Without love, material abundance becomes empty. Without love, even spiritual practice can become just another performance.

Love steadies us. It reminds us that we are more than what we own, more than what we achieve, and more than the roles we play. It teaches us that joy doesn't need to be postponed until the next promotion, the next house, or the next escape. Joy is here, in the act of loving and being loved. In living from the wholeness of who we are.

And when we finally love ourselves enough to live authentically, we can love outwardly with freedom. We stop needing the world to validate us and start simply sharing what flows through us. That love then shapes our families, our friendships, our work, and the quiet moments of our days.

This is purpose. Not a job description. Not a title. Not a role.

Purpose is love, embodied in the way we live, the way we give, and the way we see the world. From this foundation, life begins to feel different. Lighter. Radiant. Abundant. It becomes not just something to survive but something to celebrate.

And this is where my journey has brought me, into a vision of life that feels like an endless summer.

WALK 13: ENDLESS SUMMER

ENDLESS SUMMER IS NOT A SEASON. IT IS A STATE OF BEING. IT IS HOW LIFE FEELS WHEN YOU ARE TRULY FREE.

There is a rhythm to life that, once felt, cannot be unfelt. It is slow, steady, and grounded like the quiet confidence of the tide. It doesn't demand. It doesn't rush. It doesn't shout. It simply flows. That is what this chapter of my life feels like.

I call it *Endless Summer*, not because it's always warm or easy but because it's always present. It's the feeling of walking barefoot on the beach with no need to arrive. Of being fully here, fully you, without needing to prove or perform. It is what happens when all the striving stops and you finally settle into yourself.

It took me years to get here. Years of unlearning, of breaking, of remembering. I've walked through fear, ego death, identity collapse, love, grief, shame, and awakening. I've questioned everything: who I am, what I believe, how I love, what success means, what God is to me, and what I'm here for.

And now, I find myself no longer searching but simply being.

That doesn't mean I have no goals or dreams. In fact, quite the opposite. It means I no longer chase them to feel whole. I pursue them from a place of fullness and purpose, not lack. I let life unfold. I plant seeds; I show up; I trust the timing. I move in alignment, not urgency.

My life now is filled with the kind of moments I used to overlook. Quiet ones. Deep ones. Unfiltered laughter with my daughters. A still morning with a coffee. The touch of my fiancé. Song. The sun on my skin. A knowing glance. A deep breath. These are the things I used to race past. Now, they are the things I build my life around.

Love is my compass. Not the kind that confines or contracts, but the kind that expands. Love that doesn't need to be explained or labelled. Love that flows freely, in all its forms: friendship, connection, passion, truth. Love that lives not just in words, but in presence. In the way I walk through the world.

DION ELLIOTT JENSEN

I am no longer afraid of silence. No longer afraid of not being busy. No longer afraid of who I am without the mask. I've come to see that peace isn't the absence of difficulty...it's the presence of self. It's knowing who you are and choosing to return to that knowing again and again.

I've also come to understand that life isn't meant to be controlled. It's meant to be experienced. We are not here to conquer it, or fix it, or win at it. We are here to feel it. To open to it. To grow through it. And when we stop fighting the flow, we start moving with it.

This is what endless summer means to me:

Living in alignment with truth.

Letting go of urgency.

Loving without conditions.

Trusting the unfolding.

Being at home in my own skin.

Showing up fully, even when it's hard.

Laughing easily, crying freely, speaking honestly.

Giving without needing to receive.

Receiving without guilt.

Creating without attachment.

And resting without shame.

Endless summer is not a perfect life. It is a presence-filled life, one where even the shadows are welcomed, because I no longer fear what they mean. I know how to sit with discomfort now. I know how to listen to the whispers within. I no longer run from the hard things. I meet them, gently.

CONSCIOUS FOOTSTEPS

And I don't need every part of life to make sense anymore. I've found beauty in the mystery. Peace in the unanswered questions. Joy in the not knowing. There is softness here. There is space.

This book began as a private reflection. A way to make sense of my inner world as everything outside of me fell apart. I never expected it to become something I'd share. But something inside me kept saying, *Tell the truth. Tell it all. Someone out there needs it.*

So I did.

And if you're reading this, maybe that someone was you.

If you are in the unravelling…stay.

If you are in the not knowing…trust.

If you are in the becoming…keep going.

If you are tired…rest.

If you are afraid…breathe.

If you are searching…listen.

And if you are beginning to remember who you are…welcome home.

There is no single path. No final arrival point. No formula. There is only this moment. And then the next. And then the one after that. Conscious footsteps, one by one.

And with each step, more of yourself returns.

More peace.

More love.

More lightness.

More truth.

Until one day, without realising it, you find yourself walking through life like it's summer all the time, not because it's easy, but because you are free.

EPILOGUE

You made it.

Not to the end of the book, but to a pause. A breath. A moment to look back at the ground you've covered and notice what's shifted.

Maybe something small moved inside you.
Maybe something cracked open.
Maybe nothing landed just yet, and that's okay too.

These walks were never about reaching a destination. They were about presence. Awareness. Listening. Meeting yourself honestly, one step at a time.

If you've read this far, you've likely walked through parts of your own story. Noticing the echoes. Questioning old beliefs. Feeling the sting of memory, the quiet recognition of truth, the soft glow of something beginning to return.

Maybe love.
Maybe trust.
Maybe you.

There's no final chapter to healing. No clean ending to awakening. But there *is* a way of being that changes everything. A way of moving through the world with less fear,

EPILOGUE

more truth, and a heart that stays open, even after all it has endured.

This book was never about telling you how to live. It was an offering. A mirror. A rhythm you could walk alongside for a little while, until your own footsteps felt clearer again.

If anything in this book helped you remember something you'd forgotten about yourself, some part of you that had gone quiet or been waiting to return, then it was worth writing.

You don't need to start over. You don't need to be fixed.
You're not late. You're not behind.
You're just here.
And from here, the path is yours to choose.
No rush.
No rules.
Just conscious footsteps. One at a time.

ACKNOWLEDGEMENTS

To write a book is one thing. To live the words first—that's where the real work is.

This book would not exist without the people who walked with me, both in love and in loss. Whether your presence was steady, brief, or painful, you shaped me. You cracked me open. You helped me remember who I am.

To my children—thank you for being my teachers. You've shown me the deepest ache of love and the most powerful reason to keep going. You are part of every step I've taken.

To my ex-wife—your love, grace, and strength during the hardest transitions of our lives will always be something I carry with me. Thank you for the life we shared, for the home we built, and for the children we brought into this world together. Thank you for your understanding, your friendship, and your trust, not just then but now, as we continue to walk beside each other in co-parenting. I want nothing but joy, love, and fulfilment for you. You deserve all the happiness in the world and then some.

To my soon-to-be husband—thank you for your unwavering patience and the space you gave me to walk this internal path. You have been my calm, my safe harbour,

ACKNOWLEDGEMENTS

through every emotional storm. Your willingness to support me, to stand beside me as I unravelled, awakened, and became, is something I'll never take for granted. Thank you for seeing me, all of me, and loving me. I couldn't ask for a more steady, generous, and open-hearted partner to walk this life with.

To those who saw me when I couldn't fully see myself—thank you.

To the ones I hurt along the way—I hope this book reaches you, even if my words never do. I carry that too. And I honour the truth of your experience.

To those who never gave up on me, even when I pulled away—your love left a mark I'll never forget.

To the guides, creators, friends, and strangers who shared wisdom in quiet moments, whether through conversation or a passing smile—thank you for lighting the path when mine felt dark.

To my future self, who needed this book to exist—I kept going for you.

And finally, to you, the reader—thank you for showing up. For walking with me. For listening, not just to these words but to your own heart as you read them. My deepest hope is that something in these pages helped you remember who *you* are.

This is not the end.

This is the beginning of your next conscious footstep.

ABOUT THE AUTHOR

The author of *Conscious Footsteps* is a parent, a partner, and a seeker. Someone who has walked through love, loss, truth, and transformation.

Born and based in Australia, they have spent much of their life creating, building, and reflecting, often at the intersection of business, creativity, and the human spirit. Their work and words explore what it means to live with presence and purpose in a world that constantly pulls us away from both.

They were not born into a platform, nor do they speak from a stage. They write from experience: lived, felt, and sometimes wrestled with. Their words emerge from the quiet between life's noise, in those rare moments when awareness and honesty meet.

Away from writing, they find inspiration in family, nature, long walks, and conversations that go far beneath the surface. *Conscious Footsteps* is their first book.

CONSCIOUS FOOTSTEPS

DION ELLIOTT JENSEN

www.ingramcontent.com/pod-product-compliance
Lightning Source LLC
Chambersburg PA
CBHW020544080526
44583CB00013B/984